DO NOT REMOVE
CARDS FROM POCKET

A Mother's Joy

June Masters Bacher

Baker Book House
Grand Rapids, Michigan 49506

Copyright 1983 by
Baker Book House Company

ISBN: 0-8010-0852-2

Printed in the United States of America

To Bryce
Who holds my Humpty-Dumpty days together!

Contents

A Mom
By Any Other Name

I am very lucky to have a wonderful husband who wants his wife to stay home and take care of him and our two boys.

I love my job. But I wish just once someone would call me by my name, Jan, instead of "Barry's mom" or "Tommy's mom"!

—*Jan Shelton*

Overheard in a kindergarten class: "Mothers are very important. If you don't believe it, just ask them."

Letter from a Mother-to-be

Dear Unborn Child,

You and I have an advantage over everybody else in the family. We have these prep-months in which to become acquainted. So meet your mother-to-be, Child, and let's talk things over before one or the other of us takes over. Right now we're one flesh, but there's nothing status quo about being born. One of these days you'll be taking a look at the world and me and deciding whether or not you like us. We can explore the world together; but *me,* that's another matter. We'd better talk it over.

You see, the world is filled with mothers, no two of them alike. And, unfortunately, you have no choice. It seems unfair in a way, seeing that I did have some say in your make-up. Oh, I can't be sure of the exact measurements and coloring; but I can check the family tree on both sides of the family and make a calculated guess. Even if I am wrong, it will be of no consequence. Of much greater importance is what you are to accomplish — paint the greatest picture, carve the greatest statue, lead your country, or become a homemaker and mother like I. I admit a preference of the spirit over the flesh, but we'll talk about that later. We were going to talk about me.

I wish I could claim to be special—that I have soft hands and always smell of cologne. But I like to "dig in" with my hands and, to be honest, I don't even like perfumes. They make me sneeze! I wish I never raised my voice even when the washer stops in mid-cycle, my tried-and-true recipes fail, and the whole family troops in late—wearing muddy shoes. But I know in advance that I'll try to win my point by yelling when I want to pass you off as a genius and your mind turns to blubber. I'll yell again when you bring hamsters home from school for the weekend. I detest rodents. I detest snakes, too, but I *do* love dogs and cats. Can't we compromise?

I can lower my voice at an amazingly rapid pace, so depend on me to say, "I am sorry," when I am wrong; "I love you anyway," when you are; and to sing even after we've had a row. I'm not very good at lullabies, but I am practicing and loving every minute of it.

Sometimes I'm short on patience, too. I want things to happen in a hurry. Right now, it's tough waiting for your arrival. I'd better warn you that once you are here, I'll be doing the things I deplore in other mothers—pushing you along to be the first baby on the block to focus your eyes, cut a tooth, or wear a T-shirt lettered SUPER CHILD! I'll even try to push (or drag) you through college because it is what *I* want. What's more, I am apt to argue. If you say you want to be a ditch-digger, I will say, "Then be an educated one." But I like to think I am wiser (not smarter, mind you) because of my years. So trust my decisions and I'll do my utmost to cut the umbilical cord at the right stage of development.

You lucked out in some areas, though. I love reading stories, baking brownies, going to Sunday school, wading brooks . . . and I could wander aimlessly in the hills for hours, just picking wood violets or looking for elusive fairies! I love to play childish games—no matter who's winning—and I've never been one for split-second timing. A later bed check is in order if there's a good cartoon on TV or somebody needs an extra bear hug! I love chasing fireflies, going to the circus, and I think birthdays are just about the most important day of the year.

I believe in miracles, great and small. And while you and I play the waiting game, I want you to know that you, Dear Unborn Child, though a tiny miracle now, are destined to be the greatest of them all to me. We are a part of each other in a unique way. We share an experience nobody else can enter into. And, yet, it is up to us to love boundlessly, for we must bring the others in. We must unite—not divide—a family. You will have to help me in this matter, for I am apt to want to possess you. One day you, too, may experience pangs of withdrawal. So we must remember that we do not own one another. Oh, help me to remember that!

I promise to ignore those who say you're "spoiled rotten" because of the love I give you. Love does not spoil. But neither does it allow the object to go undisciplined. There may be times when you feel the rules I set down are too harsh. Bring them to the bargaining table and we'll talk. If I stand too firm, don't tell me what other mothers do. You see, God gave you to me and nobody else has quite so special a child.

And one day, with all my misgivings, maybe I'll hear those coveted words, "My mom didn't do a bad job, after all."

A New Mother's Meditation

God created a leafy bower and called it Earth.

He arched a sky above it and stuck it with stars for lighting the face of the night.

He set Earth aglow with a ripening sun and planned the seasons of sowing and growing, reaping and resting.

He planted it with friendly trees and scented it with flowers.

He sculptured powerful mountains, chiseled brooks and mighty white-capped seas.

He filled the forests and fields with warm, furry animals and set fish afloat in the seas.

It was good, God said, but unfinished. . . .

God made man in His likeness — and sensed in him a need,

So He created for man a loving mate.

And God gave them dominion over the leafy bower and all that dwelt upon it.

God endowed us all with hearts which ponder:

With whom shall we share your glory?

Who will point out the majesty of the mountains to us,

Teach us to listen for the ocean's roar,

Understand the whisper of the breeze,

Recognize the importance of the sparrow,

See the beauty of the butterfly?

Who will love us when we are old,

Remind us of what we have learned of your wisdom?

Who will share our joy and comfort us in our sorrow,
    reassure us when we are afraid,

Stand near when we are lonely,

And mend our days when they fall apart?

Who will love us, listen to us, make us feel worthwhile?

And God, in His infinite wisdom, heard our questions
and knew that His creation was unfinished.
He knew that we would grow weary and discouraged,
Need laughter and the words of love to gladden our faint
hearts and to restore our faith in ourselves.
He knew we would need bright mirrors to reflect our
better selves,
That we would grope and need hands to lead us farther
than we would be able to go alone.
He knew we would need someone to say, "You're beau-
tiful!" when we felt unloved and unlovely.
He knew our needs before we knew them ourselves.
To give us a glimpse of life and life-beyond-life, God, in
His infinite wisdom, created children —
And gave them dominion over their parents' hearts.

Thoroughly Modern
Mothers   *Well, almost. . . .*

The moms of the '80s live with many of the traditional expectations of motherhood, plus new needs and desires spurred by the women's movement and economic conditions. Women from various walks of life have contributed their personal views here to give a broader view of what it is like to be a mother today.

Read what they have to say. We think you will find yourself reflected in one of the stories, or maybe in all of them when you are having "one of those days." We think, too, that you will find mothers of today wanting the same things our mothers wanted for us and our grandmothers wanted for them. Thoroughly modern, maybe, but motherhood is here to stay!

So, little prayer,
Be on your way
To bless all mothers
On this day.

The True Meaning of "Liberated"

Being a mother, from the first joyous moment of birth to the frustrations of tending to the endless needs of a three-year-old child, has brought to me more happiness and fulfillment than I ever expected.

I am a registered nurse, and I worked for seven years before starting a family. Now I am a full-time mother, wife, and homemaker loving every moment of it and probably working harder than I ever did as a nurse.

In today's world of "the liberated woman," I finally found the true meaning of *liberated*. It is a woman who is able to enjoy the luxury of staying at home and caring for her own children and not being pressured to work outside the home due to financial needs or society's expectations.

I have two sons, a six-month-old and a three-year-old. Being their mom is the greatest pleasure of my life.

—*Julia Greeley von Seggern*

"Single" Parent Woes and Joys

I grew up as a typical all-American girl in the '50s. Some women of the '70s and '80s would say I was brain-washed because all I wanted to do was be a mommy — and a wife, of course. That was career enough for me!

But like so many other women's lives today, things didn't work out that way. I became a parent without a partner and, naturally, a working mother. My main objection to the arrangement is that there just are not enough hours in my day to be the kind of mother my children — or any child — deserve.

Besides all the tasks that any other woman handles, I work forty hours a week and sometimes manage a second or a third job. So someone else sees that my seven-year-old daughter gets to school, someone else gives her a snack afterward, and someone else hears about her exciting day, her achievements and disappointments before Mother hears. Her smashed toes and hurt feelings are tended to by someone else till I retrieve her at five o'clock. Thank God for the someone elses!

The same thing is true with my fourteen-year-old son. He has been getting himself to and from school and other activities on the city bus or by walking since he was nine.

There is no parent present at his after-school games or to help with his homework, and any news he has waits until Mom comes home from work and gets dinner started at least. In spite of it all, we adjust.

And today with my typical all-American children I sometimes find it hard to cope with soccer practice, dancing lessons, bad report cards, their occasional squabbles, a teenage boy's fist fights, computer games beeping and buzzing, loud rock-and-roll music, ripped sashes, worn out tennies, cavities, burnt fingers, spending money, transportation, and the other problems that all mothers face with or without Daddy at home.

Still, the bottom line is that I wouldn't trade my "Jack and Jill" for anyone else's. Neither would I trade the privilege of being their mother for any other career anywhere.

And when they tell me I look gorgeous and I know better; or when my son fights with another boy who says that his mom is "lazy"; or when they give me a valentine (homemade), saying their mom is the kindest, most loving, and hard-working one in the world, then I remember that all I ever wanted to be was a mommy!

—Merry Anne Nelson

There are so many ways of mothering, when one has a heartful of love.

A "Mom" to Many!

I am a mom who has the best of both worlds. I can maintain the traditional mother role because I work full time at home. I have three children of my own and I am a Monday-through-Friday mom to three to five other children with my day-care center, which is actually a substitute home for children whose mothers work.

It's not easy to convince a person who hasn't experienced six children under the age of eight that day care is a real job. There is nothing more important to me than providing a warm, secure environment for children.

There are frustrations, but not the kind you normally associate with a job. I see the results of divorces and too little time spent with children. I see the disappointed faces when parents say they will call or be there at a certain time and don't show up. I see children who spend time working on pictures and special projects and have parents who take no time to praise the efforts. These are my frustrations.

The joys are when a child comes through my door with a smile or says "Thanks" for taking her to the park or just sits on my lap of his own free will. I have an inner joy knowing that I am raising my children the way the Lord intended.

I am thankful that I am able to be at home to kiss my little one before he lies down for a nap and to share my own children's day when they return from school.

I am a mother by profession and a day-care provider by choice. I wouldn't change places with anyone!

—*Monica Harris*

The Greatest Thing

It's a privilege to be a mother of two normal, healthy sons. With all the problems and disappointments children are exposed to today and all the temptations and stimulants of today's world, I feel it is a real challenge to rear these two children as God prescribes.

I also find it a real challenge to maintain a happy and healthy home life, marriage, and career all at the same time. Nine years of interesting part-time work has balanced the full-time work of young children and child-rearing. I considered going to work during those nine years as mental health work—a time for Mom to keep in touch with reality and bring the "real world" into her home life. It was like a breath of fresh air in a world of diaper pails and Sesame Street.

I am grateful to the models I see around me in the community, at church, and at work. It's important for me to be surrounded by other women who have happy children and families and who love their work—both at home and away.

I am forever grateful for the support of the men in my life: a husband who takes delight in my successes, principals (my children's and mine) who see the value in my balancing both careers, and who support my needs and schedules.

On Mother's Day, I thought of all the joys, frustrations, and challenges of being a mother in today's world. And I realized the one thing that makes it all seem so wonderful is having a loving husband to share in it all.

So I give a hearty THAT'S RIGHT! to the saying: "The best thing a man can do for his children is to love their mother."

—Diane Kirby

In Memory...

I'm proud to share the joy of my role as "mom" during 1982.

On the evening of January 19, my sixteen-year-old son, Guy, retired with a small request. "How about a back rub, Mom?"

Back rubs are appreciated favors in our home, so I set my quilting project aside and fulfilled the request. We shared a few thoughts, and I thanked him for washing the family car. I also thanked him for a pair of oak candlesticks he'd completed at school that day and had given me. They would become a real treasure.

As I left his room, he said, "Goodnight, Mom. Thanks."

I replied, "Goodnight, son. I love you." God gave me a special joy from that bit of quality time with Guy.

The following morning was rainy and dark and, as usual, I prepared breakfast for the family. Two children were off to school and one off to work. I said good-by to Guy at the door and reminded him, as moms do, "Be careful in the rain."

The frustrations . . . my son walked out to his car that morning and out of my life. . . . His car went out of control on the rain-slick road as he returned from school. A parent's nightmare had come true in our lives.

The fatal accident made me realize how thankful I am to be "just a housewife and mom." And I'm grateful for another son, eighteen, and a daughter, thirteen, whom I love dearly.

Sometimes moms get tired of the everyday routine, but to me it's like an artist painting a picture. The single strokes may not be very exciting, but the finished masterpiece makes every stroke worthwhile!

—Terri Dahmer

Happy Memories Flash Past

She is a vision of loveliness — blue bouffant dress, patent-leather shoes, and paper mortarboard — Cheryl, our kindergarten graduate, is happy and poised.

Five years pass.

He is a portrait of boyhood manliness — shirt, tie, and plaid sportcoat, shined shoes and paper mortarboard — Darryl, our kindergarten graduate, is serene and self-confident.

Seven years rush by.

Cheryl walks to the platform again, this time to present the salutatory address as a mature and confident high-school graduate.

My husband says if we move to California there is a remote possibility Darryl may march in the Tournament of Roses parade. I dismiss it as "impossible."

We move to California.

Darryl marches in the Rose Parade twice with the Orange Glen Band. He also participates in the moving of the Liberty Bell on January 1, 1976.

Five months pass.

Darryl, wearing cap and gown together with other senior band members, takes his turn directing the band at high-school graduation.

Now, both have gone on to wear other caps and gowns, having attained higher educational goals.

Between kindergarten and college graduations there
have been

Brownies,
  Cub Scouts,
  Sunday school,
    4-H,
    P.T.A.,
      tantrums,
        dog obedience classes,
        homework,
          orthodontia,
          piano lessons,
          car pools,
            bronchitis,
            poor grades,
            honor rolls,
              an emergency midnight trip to the
                hospital in a snow storm,
            school plays,
              bicycles,
              moodiness,
                choral programs,
                learning to drive,
                a broken arm,
                ice skating,
                X-rays,
                  Christmas programs,
                  band concerts,
                    physical therapy,
                    first jobs,
                      Carribean cruise,
                      community college,

selling candy and cookies and magazines,
learning to bake,
  upset stomachs,
    birthday parties,
      measles,
        driving tests,
        friends,
          scholarships,
           snow forts,
           mumps,
             family celebrations,
              chicken pox,
                newspaper routes,
                Girls' State,
                 first dates,
                  proms,
                   cheerleading,
                     instrument practice,
                    school games,
                     exhilaration,
                       yearbook editor,
                       baby sitting,
                       band camp,
                         earning money,
                          sibling rivalry,
                           career plans,
                            career plans, change of
                     — and *love!*

Now it's "Happy Birthday" sung on the telephone,
and "Hi, Mom, I'm coming home this weekend."
    I'm thankful that God has permitted me to participate
in the kaleidscope of trials, triumphs, frustrations, and
joys of motherhood.

—Ernestine Seefeldt

"Holding the Bag" Who? Me?

I had the option of aborting this child. I did not. I loved his father and chose to be married. But within two years his father died. I still remember the awful bitterness of being left "holding the bag."

My son is now fifteen years old and motivates a multitude of emotions within me. I delight in his pride of manhood. I am amused at his wry acceptance that at this point girls consider him a creep!

I am relieved that we share a common vocabulary and am aggravated over his politics. I am dismayed that some of his habits are twins to mine, but I am cheered at my inability to dominate him.

I admire his perseverance and growl at his obstinancy. I am in awe of his dreams and ambitions.

The greatest of my emotions, however, is thankfulness in my heart for this "bag" I was left to carry. There always have been and there always will be treasures within it.

—S. McRae

A Smile Makes It All Worthwhile!

Aahhh, the joys of motherhood. They are many, indeed.

The things I heard said when I carried my child within me were all true. One of them was, "Sleep now as much as possible because when the baby's born, you will have no opportunity." This one couldn't be more true. My new son is only two months old now, but I can tell you that it feels like four or more.

I remember clearly the many days I walked around like a zombie trying to concentrate on where I was going or what I was trying to accomplish. Those middle-of-the-night feedings were the real culprits of my destitute state of mind.

One morning at 3:00 A.M. when I was walking the floor, hoping my son would nod out before I did, something wonderful happened! I blinked to make sure. . . .

Was it? Yes, it was! A smile. A real person was inside that sleepless little body — someone who thinks, loves, cares, and, above all else, knows I exist.

All that time I had been wondering if my energies were accomplishing anything, but then I knew. He really is someone.

Since that night, Nicholas John has laughed and cooed, telling me how much he loves me and appreciates my endless hours of rocking. This, by far, is reason enough to keep going and anticipating the future and all it holds for us.

I know motherhood can only get better now. I have been through the worst part, and I know soon he'll be sleeping through the night!

—Annette Downey

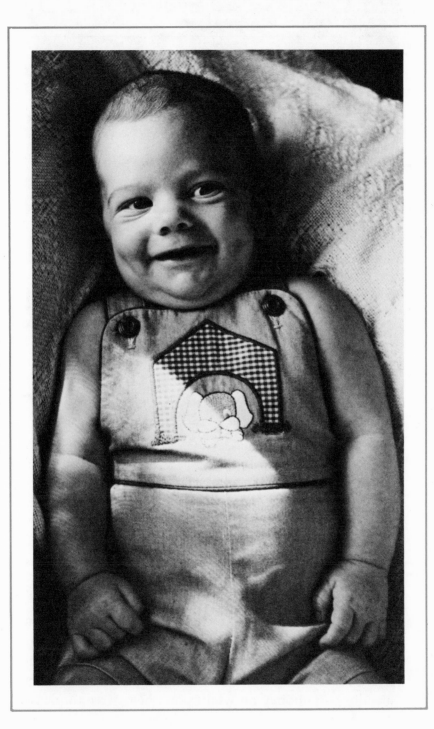

Living for Tomorrow

When I attended college in the '70s, one of the favorite philosophies dealt with living for today. It went something like this: "Live only for today because yesterday is but a memory and tomorrow only a dream."

That all sounded well and good at the time, but that was a long time before I had three boys. When I became a mom, I discovered that my todays were no longer comprised of late-night parties and sleeping until noon, spending my money on whims, and being free to please

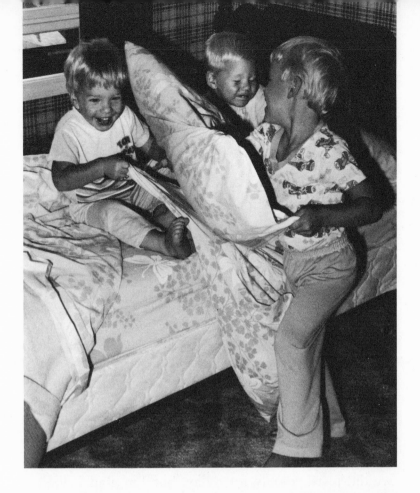

myself. I traded that for days of running to the pediatrician, doing three loads of laundry a day, spending my money on baseballs and Hot Wheel cars, and staying up late to wash the crayon marks off the walls and the mud tracks off the carpets.

My boys frequently turn their noses up at my gourmet meals, refuse to wear my sewing efforts, and insist on making mischief when I'm on the phone long distance.

What keeps me going and keeps my attitude optimistic is not always my todays, but my yesterdays and my tomorrows, my memories and my dreams. When today isn't all that I would like it to be, I can't toss in the towel. What I do is stop and remember the day my little mischief makers were born, the first time they said "Mommy" with all that love in their eyes, the first Christmas presents they made and wrapped for me "all by ourselves." Sometimes my yesterdays are what make today worthwhile. And sometimes my thoughts of tomorrow are what carry me through my today!

When I look at my sons who have just used an entire first aid box to doctor the dog, I try not to see $6.98 worth of Band-aids and antiseptic wasted. I look at it as practice for the future, or I try to.

Three brothers having food fights at the table, water fights in the bath, and pillow fights in the bedroom try my patience, but I put up with it. I know what value those brothers will be to each other in the future. Rivals for my time and attention now, they will be each other's best friends and closest allies later on. And "tomorrow," whenever it comes, when their father and I are no longer on this earth to care for them, they will have each other and a lot of happy memories and dreams because we did not live today just for ourselves.

Today might be easier financially and emotionally if we did just live only for today, but I'm glad I don't. I think the results of that lifestyle might be very lonely when tomorrow comes.

Personally, I look forward to tomorrow. I have a stake in it — three stakes named Chris, Shaun, and Tom.

—*Margie McDonnell*

So You Want to Be a Mother?

You want to hear about motherhood? I am qualified to tell you about it.

I have been a mother for over thirty years. My husband and I have raised six children. Our youngest is ten years old. We are grateful that we finally got a mellow one. God knew that we were too battle-weary for another high-spirited one!

I had morning sickness for twenty years. My eyes still wear dark circles from lack of sleep. The babies all had colic (only at night).

I almost forgot what hot food tasted like. The babies slept soundly until the food was on the table, then, as if an alarm rang, each howled for my attention.

Our dining room wall has six layers of wallpaper. We redid it after each child learned to feed her- or himself. It now looks strange to see it without pablum dripping down. I think I liked it better the other way. It had more personality.

I walked through jelly and spilled milk so many years, I still walk funny.

When one child came down with mumps, measles, chicken pox, a cold, or the flu, they all followed suit.

During those years I felt that there were more patients in our home than at Palomar Hospital.

When the children were ill, I nursed them with loving care. When I was ill, I had to keep moving.

And then there were the teen years. Look at a charming little two-year-old sometime and try to guess what he or she will be like as a teen. One could not believe that they will want to drive the family car at age fourteen, that they might feel that it is dumb to deprive them of such a simple thing until they are sixteen — two years of verbal battle.

We somehow lived through the broken hearts, broken bones, concussions, scrapes, bruises, pneumonia, and tonsillectomies. The amount of money we paid for their medical care handsomely supported our family doctor and kept Palomar Hospital in the black.

But, one by one, they grew up. I remember then how incomplete I felt as each one went away. When they all return for a family celebration, I feel complete again.

Recently we were all together for a birthday celebration. They were all so happy to be together. Laughter, banter, and corny jokes filled our house for hours. When the older boys left, my husband and I agreed that we pitied childless couples who had never had their home filled with that kind of noise.

The years that were so busy with baking cookies, planning birthday parties, coloring Easter eggs, filling Christmas stockings, helping with homework, attending P.T.A. meetings and little league ball games, mending jeans, sewing dresses, talking to them, listening to them, offering advice and kissing away the pain from their "Oowies!" were meaningful years of treasure. I would not trade them for the highest paying position in the nation.

I recently had surgery. The first thing I saw when I awoke was my beautiful children, their faces filled with

love, tears, and concern. It would have been dreadful had they not been there.

I thank God for granting to me the most marvelous of all titles — Mother.

— Marie Baldwin

Who Says I'm Wrong!

Raising children is never quite what you thought it would be. One never imagines the sleepless nights — one after the other. One never imagines the loads of laundry — one after the other — either.

Then, there's your screaming toddler, right in the middle of a check-out line in a busy store, with everybody glaring at you, thinking, "Why doesn't she make him stop?" And when you "do something" about it, they're thinking, "How horrible — punishing that poor, helpless child."

The hardest part by far is everybody telling you, "You're raising your children all wrong." Then they proceed to tell you how you should be doing it. By the day's end, you have twenty methods to toilet train a child and twenty people telling you that none of them will work. "You're doing it all wrong," they say.

Then come all the decisions. "Mom, may I walk downtown with Joyce and Sue? Their moms let *them*." "Mom, can I go off-road dirt-biking with Mark and Todd? *Everybody's* going." You want your children to live life to its fullest, but you want them to live to adulthood also!

Yet, with all the trials and tribulations of childraising, I would not have it any other way! Nothing can compare, surely, to hearing your baby's first laugh or first word, seeing your baby's first step, enjoying your child's first friend, and sharing your child's first camping trip or first trip to Disneyland.

There is something so immensely rewarding about this tiny human being—with no experience at all, just waiting to be taught all the wonders of the world . . . to develop respect and consideration for all the things of life—including himself or herself—and to be guided into leading an intelligent, happy life. And maybe one of the rewards is the knowing that there can be no one "right" way for mothers to handle the awesome assignment!

—Cathy Peterson

When God thought of mother,
He must have laughed with satisfaction,
And framed it quickly—
So rich, so deep, so divine,
So full of soul, power, and beauty,
Was the conception.

—Henry Ward Beecher

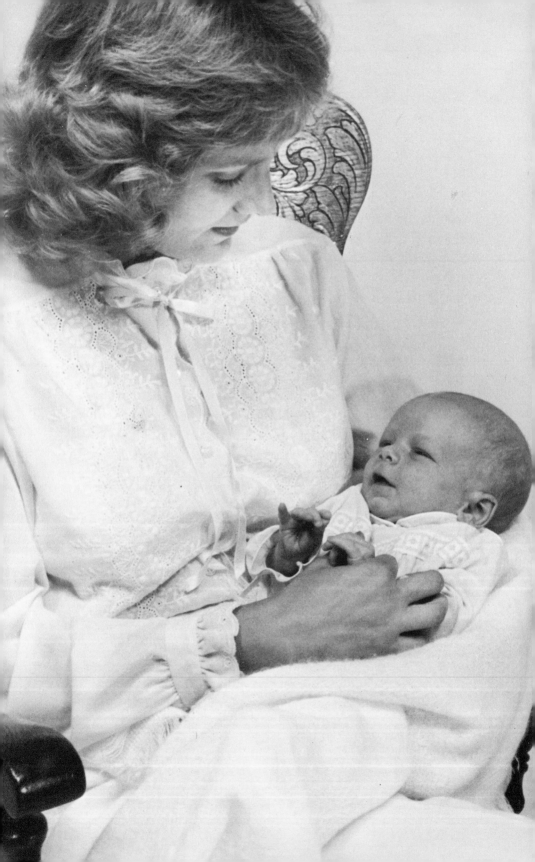

From These Days to Those

I just sit here rocking
My new baby son . . .
The washing is waiting,
The dusting, undone.
Time somehow I've managed
(I'm not sure just how)
For memory-making
I'm using right now.
From these days to those days
(When he's up and gone)
I'll save work and thinking
For when I'm alone.
Then, after my cleaning,
I'll sit in this chair
And rock with the feel of
My cheek on his hair.

To be read some day when growing-up seems long to you — again when growing-up seems long to the child — and you are both sure to remember "Ollie."

Good-bye, Little Boy

In a little white house with green shutters, surrounded by a jungle of flowers just right for crawling through, there lived a family of three. At least, there were three that most people knew about — a mother, a daddy, and one small boy named Ollie. Actually, there were *two* small boys, only nobody had seen the other one, except Ollie.

Now Ollie wondered how this could be. His friend was there all the time, doing exactly the same things that Ollie did, at exactly the same time. He was like a shadow, a colored shadow, for his hair was curly and yellow like Ollie's, his eyes were after-the-rain blue like Ollie's, and he had exactly the same number of fingers and toes, all of them fat and pink. Ollie liked him better than any of the other boys and girls who came to visit, maybe because he held his spoon in his left hand, like Ollie, when he ate his cereal, or maybe because he looked so much like himself. Sometimes when Ollie looked into Mother's mirror, he wasn't sure at all whether it was himself looking back or whether it was his friend.

Ollie told Daddy about his friend, and Daddy searched for him under the bed where Ollied loved to hide, in the laundry basket where "Fluff" hid her kittens, and in the rhubarb patch. Daddy searched for the little boy every place — but one. He didn't look for him right beside Ollie, and that's where he always was!

Ollie told mother about his friend, too, and he gave her a hint. "He's right beside me, Mother." Mother looked and looked, and she said she could almost see him. Almost, but not quite. "Does he have a name?" Mother wondered. "We can't have two Ollies, you know."

Ollie thought about the name for a long, long time — maybe two days. He would lie awake after his prayers thinking, as he looked at the teddy-bear night light, that a big boy like himself should have a name, but it could not be Ollie. And then he thought of a very wonderful name, a name filled with all the world's magic. "Good night, *Little Boy*," he whispered.

Ollie and Little Boy were up early the next morning. They washed their hands together, and Ollie held the towel while Little Boy dried. When they entered the sunny breakfast nook, Mother smiled her good-morning smile and said, "What would you like for breakfast, Ollie?" Ollie smiled *his* good-morning smile and said, "Both of us would like cereal." So Mother put down two white bowls, two pale pink napkins, and two spoons for left-handed boys.

It was a wonderful day, more wonderful somehow because Little Boy had a name. The two of them chased butterflies beneath the flowering plum tree. They caught a green lady frog, but they let her go right away because she told them she had babies that needed attention. They talked briefly with a honeybee who was painting his legs yellow with tulip pollen, and they teased a baby-sitter for a lady robin into showing where the nest was hidden in the Winesap appletree boughs. And there followed a whole summer full of wonderful days.

Ollie told Mother all about the things he and Little Boy were doing, and sometimes as Mother listened, she asked questions. *What happened to the butterflies?* They disappeared, he told her. *The lady frog?* He didn't know, but the green babies were hopping all over the raspberry patch. The robins had hatched, learned to fly and to talk fairly well, and then flown away. Mother nodded. "Yes, Ollie. Things change," she said.

And things went right on changing. The Winesap apples ripened. The tulips shook off their summer ruffles and twisted themselves into tight little green seedpods. The leaves on the raspberry bushes turned to deep gold. Each day Ollie and Little Boy spent the time apart now — always near to each other, to be sure, but each doing what he wished to do, alone. Ollie often left Little Boy when he went with Daddy downtown, too. "Good-by, Little Boy," he would say as he and Daddy rode away. Little Boy didn't seem to mind. He would wave and smile and would be waiting when Ollie returned.

"Ollie," Mother said one night at prayer time, "soon now you will be going to school. What will you do with Little Boy while you are away?"

"Oh, he'll have to go with me."

Ollie didn't see much of Little Boy during those busy days of shopping for plaid shirts, a cherry-red lunch pail, and a box of fat crayons. He was so busy that he almost forgot to take Little Boy with him when he went for his just-before-school haircut. What's more, Little Boy didn't behave very well in the barber shop. He was afraid of the *whrrrrr* of the clippers, and he kept fussing about hair getting down the neck of his t-shirt.

The day the big lemon-colored school bus came for them, Little Boy disappeared. Ollie, who was ready to go at least fifteen minutes ahead of time, wondered what could be the matter with his friend. Little Boy played with his cereal. He couldn't find his crayons. He forgot to brush his teeth. Then, he just up and disappeared for a long time.

Ollie was tired before they finally got on the bus. He stayed tired all day.

Mother was waiting at the gate when the school bus brought Ollie home from his very first day at school. "Hello, fellows! How did you get along?"

"Well, I got along fine. But Little Boy, well, he got lost . . ." Ollie hesitated, hoping Mother would not feel sad. "I looked and I looked for him, but I couldn't find him anywhere. So I had to come home," he squared his shoulders, "all by myself."

Mother did look sad, but she looked proud, too. "Good-by, Little Boy," she said.

And so it is. In the little white house with green shutters, surrounded by a jungle of flowers just right for crawling through, there lives a family of three — a mother, a daddy, and one small boy named Ollie.

To Talk About Together

1. Do you know anyone who invented an imaginary playmate when he or she was little?
2. Why do you think Ollie invented Little Boy?
3. Have you ever felt lonely and wanted to have more friends?
4. Why do you think Ollie began to forget Little Boy as he grew older?
5. Ollie's mother "played along" with the idea of his imaginary friend. Do you think she knew why he invented Little Boy?
6. Why do children, or even older people, need friends?

Childhood Wisdom

Small child, let's go and find the spring.
Together you and I
Can find its secrets on the wings
Of breezes passing by.
We'll count the daisies in the lane
And maybe pick a few,
We'll drink the nectar from each rose
And sail the seas of dew.
Then you'll recall when you've grown tall
How every living thing
Is born anew each time it finds
The secrets of a spring.
So gather memories and dreams
And know that dreams come true,
When you remember Wisdom once
Was just a child like you.

Help Me, Lord!

My mother and I used to play a little game called "What if?" What if I should come home and be unable to find my key? What if I came home and found my parents gone or saw someone else inside the house? What if a stranger asked me to ride, offered me candy, or tried to force me into an automobile? These were the questions Mama asked to assist me in learning wise precautions.

"Why don't you ever ask what I'd do if I met up with a wolf? Or somebody offered me a poison apple or left me out in the woods like Hansel and Gretel?" I asked my mother one day.

"Because you are ready to go to school now and you probably won't have to face those problems."

And so we went on playing the game by her rules until I answered each question to my mother's satisfaction. Then, one day I popped her a question: "What if," I asked slowly, "none of these things work out?"

"Never hesitate to ask for help," she answered.

We all face the dangers of a world wider than our backyards when we venture away from home and start our own families. The dangers can be neither avoided nor denied. But my mother did a good job of helping me face up to such dangers in advance. And, one by one, I encountered almost every situation she prepared me for — situations which threatened me physically, financially, or emotionally. Yes, they continue to crop up ... but I know what to do.

Today I am facing a "What if?" with my own child. *So help me, Lord!*

What My Mother Always Told Me

M others most often *do* know best (and generally tell us children so). Not that I believed this to be the case until I entered the arena of "mothering" myself. Then what a boon to have a born list-maker like Mama!

When my own dumpling baby came to live with my husband and me, his arrival sent shock waves into all my preconceived notions of exactly how parents were to behave. The first problem: I did not know how *babies* behaved. The second problem: I lacked the nine-months' preparation time (which well-meaning friends assured me gave the insight and understanding I lacked). You see, we brought our new baby home from the courtroom instead of the hospital. That's how it happens when you graft a new member onto the family tree instead of "planting the seed."

What to do? My mother knew all the answers, and had just seven suggestions:

1. Make the home his "social environment."
2. Teach the skills of kindness.
3. Praise his process more than the outcome.
4. Take every day a bite at a time.
5. Avoid labels and comparisons.
6. Let him help.
7. Love without condition!

A Mother's Quote Book

God could not be everywhere and therefore He created mothers.

—Old Jewish Saying

Nature's loving is the watchful mother.

—Bulwer

The mother in her office holds the key of the soul; and it is she who stamps the coin of character and makes who would be savage, but for her cares, a Christian! Then crown her queen of the world.

—Old Play

The mother's heart is the child's schoolroom.

—H. W. Beecher

How kind is the sieve of time! It always leaves only the tenderest memories on top of the strainer.

Every child born into the world is a new thought of God, an ever-fresh and radiant possibility.

—*Kate Douglas Wiggin*

Even he that died for us on the cross, in the last hour, in the unutterable agony of death, was mindful of His mother, as if to teach us that this holy love should be our last worldly thought—the last point of earth from which the soul should take its flight to heaven.

—*Longfellow*

The tendrilled vine of tender hands
Meant, "Yes, Child, Mother understands."
So my small hands within hers curled
Were holding fast a childhood world
Made safe by words (Mothers are wise!)
Until the Sandman closed my eyes. . . .
Oh! how I miss that trusted hand
That guided me to Slumberland.

The Unfinished Curtains

Once upon a time there was a mother who never made curtains. She never made slipcovers or pajamas or Halloween costumes either. She was a disgrace to three generations of seamstresses. Not that she didn't try! When the first baby was expected, the grandmother made it very clear that the child must not be born until the mother had created some baby clothes with her very own hands. Cleverly, the mother designed a tiny flannel dressing gown, colored both pink *and* blue, so that it wouldn't be necessary to make more than one.

The grandmother was disappointed that the baby was a boy. "Girls are such fun to sew for!" However, she mentioned hopefully that the nursery needed some brightening up and suggested that some homemade gingham curtains would do the trick. Privately, the mother felt that the nursery was gloriously bright enough with just the little blond boy in it, but reluctantly she agreed to go shopping for the blue-checked fabric.

Now the fabric stores were dread places to the mother, for she had spent most of her childhood in them, lost and miserable, hidden by rows and rows of bolts of fabric, while the grandmother and *her* mother pursued their

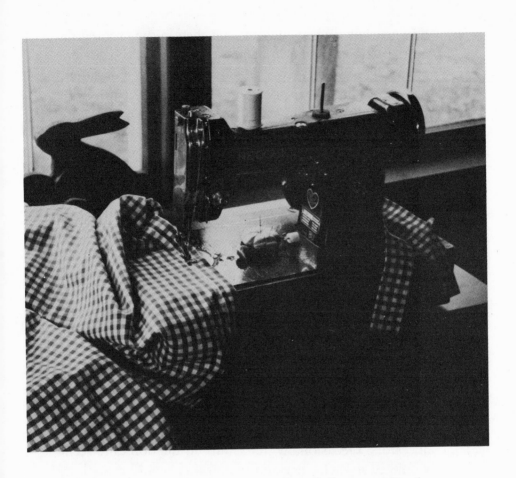

favorite hobby. They would stand and figure endlessly how to get the garment they wanted from the least amount of material possible and then more hours, it seemed, matching the fabric with zippers, thread, and buttons. The child would be told twenty times, "Just a few more minutes, Dear."

So the gingham curtains were dutifully begun, only to be set aside whenever anything else the least bit more important came along. The mother and son particularly enjoyed walks outdoors when the weather was brisk and would return home rosy-cheeked from the morning's jaunt and then take a hearty afternoon nap. Then it was time to cook and eat dinner, and then in the evening the mother certainly couldn't neglect the father just for some sewing, could she? Always there were friends to visit and cookies to bake and poems to write and, of course, the laundry was never finished.

The grandmother's hopes soared when it was revealed that a second baby was expected. Surely with a family of two children, the mother would learn to sew, bake bread, and maybe make jam. But alas, the second child was also a boy and did not require any ruffled pinafores. Once, in a moment of determination and eagerness to please, the mother searched for the box containing the unfinished curtains. She gazed at the wrinkled mess for a long moment and decided to wash diapers instead. Maybe someday she would learn to sew like a "good mother" ought. Maybe someday she would be a "complete mother."

The years passed. The children grew beautifully without homemade clothes and lived quite happily in a room with storebought curtains instead. The mother was always busy but hardly ever in the traditional ways of her ancestors. Occasionally her failure in the domestic scene would overwhelm her and the mother would cry a little and resolve to learn home canning, bread making, aerobic dancing, and something called "stretch 'n sew." But when the time came for classes to begin, the mother always turned up at the local junior college, taking chemistry, biology, and algebra. She felt very smart, but she was never very useful.

When the younger boy entered kindergarten and the mother went to work full time, the good Lord provided yet another chance for success at homemaking. Imagine the grandmother's anticipation of a baby girl at last! The mother did feel that the Lord was trying to tell her something, and she made a concerted effort to keep house in the traditional manner. The husband always noticed the change to spic-and-span when a baby was expected, and in later years was known to remark wistfully about having still another baby in order to get the house clean.

The mother did become proficient in most areas, but put off the sewing decision until the baby came. The whole family eagerly awaited the arrival of Little Number Three, and the grandparents were particularly eager for a girl since there were no granddaughters yet.

At last the day arrived and the mother, after considerable struggle, was delivered of a strapping, eight-pound, bright-red, bouncy baby—*boy*. The doctor and the nurse in attendance were mystified to hear her murmur, "Thank you, Lord. You knew I didn't want to finish those curtains."

And she never did.

—Connie Bain Petersen

What is a boy?
The future of America
with a frog in his pocket!

On Clocks and Calendars

Timing is the thing. You know that. But last night there was this marvelous children's program on at 8:30. Eight o'clock is bedtime, but this program was *so* special and their teacher said watch. So, "Well—maybe—but just this once!" And you may be right.

Now, in making the catastrophic decision, you thought only of the half hour's delay in bedtime schedule—and forgot that 8:30 is the beginning time. You enjoyed the hour-long program last night yourself and didn't have the heart to send them to bed. So they sleep in a little this morning.

The children survive. You may not. Rest assured that dedicated eaters of cold cereals will demand oatmeal and four-minute eggs for breakfast. They'll opt for hot cocoa instead of the usual milk. Buttons will fall off. Zippers will stick. And static electricity will claim everything in sight. The shower head will stick, too, until you go in to unstick it. Then it will let go in pent-up fury undoing yesterday's trip to the beauty shop. The twins will gargle with Daddy's shaving lotion. Ants will invade the sugar bowl, and your daughter will spray her hair with the insecticide. You can't find the emergency poison-treatment chart and when you do, you can't find the victim. Toast will burn and set off the fire detector.

You look at the clock. They're late for school! *They* look at the calendar. "It's Saturday, Mother."

Remembering with Love

Did I add the cream of tartar,
Beat the egg whites "to a peak"?
What's a "little pinch of soda"?
Oh, I wish a book could speak!
Did I grease the tube pan "lightly"?
Just how long should "one dash" be?
"Do not open the oven. . . ."
Is it rising? I can't see!
How much is a "double handful"?
Can't a "lump" be any size?
It's small wonder Mother named it:
"Special Cake — A Sure Surprise"!
If I don't look, I'll regret it;
If I do, it's sure to fall;
Either way it's fifty-fifty;
Her "Surprise" will shock us all!

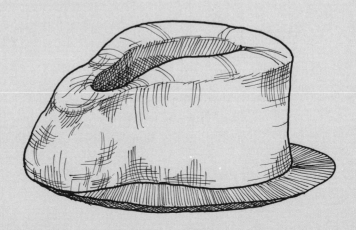

Myths or Truths — Which?

(Mothers Speak Out)

Myth: *"Twins" are never quite as intelligent as other children.*

Truth: My twins had the highest I.Q.'s in the family!

Myth: *"Identical twins" think alike, talk alike, and are closer than fraternal twins or other brothers and sisters.*

Truths: I have an identical twin. Neither of us felt we had a distinct identity of our own. Even our names sounded the same. We refused to dress alike or even be seen together — not that it helped. Even our boy friends couldn't tell us apart!

Myth: *Fraternal twins" bear none of the stigma of twins.*

Truth: The worst part about being a fraternal twin is hearing people say, "But you don't *look* alike!" Or, "But the *other* one can do this!" You get to feeling guilty because you *are* different.

Myth: *"Only children" are lonely, spoiled, and disadvantaged.*

Truth: I grew up as an only child and was never lonely. Mother read to me; I was allowed to participate in adult conversations; and I was resourceful, creative, and imaginative — qualities I noticed lacking in my playmates. I shared more, too.

Myth: *The "first child" bears the burden of helping bring up younger brothers and sisters.*

Truth: My older child — a daughter — washed her hands of her siblings! The second was a regular "mother hen."

Myth: *The "middle child" is ignored completely, the first one being a novelty and the last one being a miracle.*

Truth: Don't you believe it! I wound my older brother around my little finger and dominated my baby sister.

Myth: *The "youngest child" is never made to toe-the-mark the way the older ones had to do.*

Truth: In our family, the opposite was true. We brought the first four up when permissiveness was *the* way. By the time number five came along, we saw our mistakes and laid down the law!

Myth: *"Only boys" are effeminate.*

Truth: Six girls and one boy in my brood prepares me to say there's at least *one* exception. Our boy could throw the hardest softball in town. He ignored all girls who couldn't fill in as shortstop.

Myth: *"Only girls" tend to be shy.*

Truth: Mine was vaccinated with a phonograph needle!

Myth: *The "adopted child" suffers an identity crisis.*

Truth: We have four children: three are adopted, and the other was born to us. Our adopted boy is indifferent to information regarding his natural parents. One of our adopted girls is objectively interested in a Where-did-I-come-from? sort of way. The other says, "I bet I was supposed to be born in this family and somebody got the records mixed up." And the child born to us worries because, "You didn't pick *me* out!"

Myth: *The "younger parent" enjoys children more.*

Truth: I was scared to death for fear I'd break our first baby. I was scared to death for fear the second baby would break the bank. Ten years passed and along came the "bonus baby." I just relaxed and enjoyed every special moment.

Myth: *The "older parent" finds a late-arriving child a problem.*

Truth: Just the opposite! We had time. We had money. We had more love!

Presented by a Child

The flower shops are lovely now;
My feet just beg to turn
And go inside where I can buy
Some roses wrapped in fern.
Red roses are her favorites,
But they must cost a lot—
I count my pennies hopefully,
But ten are all I've got. . . .

I'll look for sweetbriars by the road
(They're roses growing wild)
For mothers like the simple things
Presented by a child.
She'll take this single-petal rose
And put it on a shelf
Then smile and say, "It's special for
You chose it by yourself."

I know she'll like my flower so
I'll put away this dime
So I can buy a gift-shop gift
For her some other time.

Propriety

Dear Mother and Dad,

Well, here's the news you've been waiting for. You're going to be grandparents!

I wanted to tell you the minute we learned from the doctor, but something told me to wait until we could sort of get things straight. When we set down the hard-and-fast rules about parent and grandparent roles before, we were talking about other families. Now it all looks different, because we're talking about *us*.

It is better that we have an understanding now. Since all of us are more comfortable with rules, maybe we'd better work out a few. Do you agree that there should be job descriptions for the two of you and the two of us? I'm going to need you, Mother and Dad—need you very much—but maybe those needs should be defined, for you have some needs, too!

We'll all be changing roles, you know. I guess it's as hard for you to think of yourselves as grandparents as it is for me to think of myself as a mother. You probably still think I'm in the growing-up stage. Well, a few years back, I was rebelling against that, but I guess the doctor's news turned my thinking around. We, all of us, have some growing to do! Right now, for instance, I am torn between rushing to the telephone to shout the good news and selfishly savoring my "mother moment" all alone.

But a moment is all it is! I must come out of my pink-and-blue cocoon and plan with you. It is essential, for this baby is family property with tremendous binding power. But *we* must remain friends. All of us hold propriety.

Here are some suggestions. You deserve equal time, so temper these with suggestions of your own and we'll compromise.

Suggestion 1: Let's agree that there is no maximum dosage on love. If anybody comes out with a book that refutes that, let's toss it in the fire and use the "horse sense" you brought me up with. Of course, love doesn't mean coddling, over-indulging, or keeping a growing child in a baby-bunting suit. Love is a growth vitamin!

Suggestion 2: The two of us will have to be first in command, even if the two of you feel we're not ready to take over. Now, this is not to say we won't need help. Right now, you'd be lying awake worrying if you knew how unprepared I personally feel. But let us try, for as the "experts" put it, ultimately it is the parents who are responsible for "the total child." We'll learn. So help us!

Suggestion 3: About visiting time—this gets sticky. You brought me up in a family circle that was both wide and warm, but you left no doubt that home was the hub. There was security in that knowledge (still is!), the same kind of security I want this baby to have. Let *him* pig out on your baking powder biscuits; let *her* in on your secret of those fat lemon meringue pies. And I wouldn't have either of them miss your cotton-candy Christmases for the world!

It's just that we don't want this grandchild caught between your desires and ours. Come to think of it, one of the reasons for this letter is to make sure we beginning parents don't put *you* in that position either. If either of us ever takes you for granted as built-in baby-sitters, kick us in the shins, will you? Knowing you, you will want to help—even enjoy it—but you are not expected to work so many hours to qualify.

Suggestion 4: Let's not be over-protective. I used to eat raw sweet potatoes on the sly and roll my long stockings below my knees the minute I was out of sight. I somehow doubt that any of the childhood illnesses I came down with resulted from those violations. No amount of "sound advice" is going to keep the little ones from experimenting. And come to think of it I'd rather have to splint up a few chipped bones than have them miss out on all the fun, wouldn't you? I've known some Grandmas and Grandpas who rubbed the children's chests with Vicks salve the minute they, themselves, sneezed. Promise not to do that, and I'll promise to learn how to use a fever thermometer and to watch for the signs that spell trouble.

Suggestion 5: Give me an opportunity to show you that I have a reasonable amount of judgment. And you don't have to prove your point to me. I grew up under it, you know, and it will amaze you to discover how much has rubbed off on me.

Suggestion 6: I saved this one until last. Maybe it shouldn't be included except that it's important and you were always great at taking my "importances" as big business. This has to do with the nasty little word called *jealousy.* You see, this baby is so special—the most special thing that has ever happened to me—that I feel a peculiar selfishness building up. I am ready to share this joy; but, frankly, not the object of it! Will you try to understand? Remember how it was with my new dolls

until you taught me to share them with pride? Stranger yet is the vague feeling that maybe this baby will take *you* from *me*. So I guess I'm not quite through with being your daughter. So love me, but don't let me stop growing.

You're going to be wonderful grandparents, warm, loving, and supportive. By the way, can you keep the baby next October 1st, our anniversary?

Woman-to-Woman

My dear daughter,

Well, how could anything that "is to be expected" hit me so unexpectedly? I am talking of the news that you are "expecting." I'm rather glad you chose to write. Being the sentimental silly that I am I'd have blubbered. I did anyway, but in privacy. Babies do that to me. Isn't it great that they make no-run mascara these days?

About the suggestions, let me assure you there will be no problems that the four of us can't negotiate. It's good for you to get matters of propriety off your chest the way you did and no apologies are necessary. You should have seen the rules I set down when I learned you were on the way—a bona fide (I told myself) contract, in triplicate (one for each set of grandparents and one for us as evidence). Well, you were smart enough to mail yours!

Dad will insist that we call tonight, I'm sure. He'd gone to work when the mail came, and I wouldn't want the company to think he's slacking off this close to retirement. He wouldn't be worth his salt if he knew he was about to have a grandson. Oh, yes, he'll insist the baby will be a boy, but you and I know better. He was sure in your case, too, but you and I pulled it off, didn't we though?

But before we all start talking at once tonight—you know, about names (you forgot to mention that, so surely you are open to suggestions) and agreeing on our roles as grandparents—I want you and me to have one of those woman-to-woman talks. Oh, not about the birds and the bees, you obviously know about that!

First, though, I want you to know that I've called everybody on the block and my prayer chain. They're all busy calling everybody else, so I'll have a minute's peace for this letter. I told them I needed *things* more than advice—you know, getting the crib and highchair back (I gave them away when you outgrew them), some brownie recipes (I'll gain back those pounds I shed at the spa, being a stir-and-taste cook like I am), and suggesting safety pins and Pampers just in case they decide to give me a grandmother's shower. You didn't mind if I told, did you? It's my moment, too.

I'm not going to be foolish like some I know, though. One of the Pink Ladies at the hospital told me she has six grandchildren and every time one of her children springs another on her she emerges from her cocoon and becomes a butterfly. Well, even though this is my first, I'll be no butterfly. I'm not ready to spin and die, let me assure you. I'm busy and involved and I intend to stay that way—except for time out to make sunsuits, repaint the nursery, sort out the button box, see about renewing season tickets to the zoo, sitting whenever you need us, family meals, little things like that.

But about that talk. Let there be no doubt that I can accept the new role thrust on me. Trust me to handle grandmotherhood. Qualifications? Well, I raised you, didn't I? And, believe me, you were no push-over. Your father specified a *boy* and sometimes I felt he got what he asked for! Some days you could shatter glass at sixty paces with your *screeching*; you always insisted that I bathe you and the dog at the same time; you chose earthworms for pets; and you never did get your boy-girl roles sorted out. One day you were a fairy princess in need of a costume, the next a professional gymnast trying to conquer the parallel bars. So, yes, I can manage, be this baby dreamer or powerhouse.

I'll not caution you about your health. Your obstetrician knows your need for additional calcium (You *are* drinking plenty of milk, aren't you?). And you and Hank will have to decide on feedings and schedules. It may surprise you to learn dads know as much as mom about mixing formulas, and schedules won't work anyway. Babies bring travel clocks along, and I have yet to see a parent who knows how to silence the alarm. I do want to caution you about setting up a list of expectations, however. It's hard to accept, but these little ones aren't really our property. They just board with us for approximately twenty years. *Then* comes the hard part—letting go.

Confusing? Maybe some pictures would help (mental ones for I don't want to be one of those grandmothers who shows reel after reel of home movies marked "Baby

Trying to Turn Over"). I'm seeing these pictures myself today, wondering if I handled things right and asking if I'll do better this time around. You went through the perils of babyhood fine and, contrary to *your* grandmother's admonitions, you didn't drown in the fish pond, obviously. But I set an unrealistic goal much too early of how you were to act, which schools you should attend, and who should be your friends; and I was determined to bulldoze my way past the goal line. I checked the family background of all your girl friends and made suspicious noises about dates with boys who were too popular. Remember the night you rebelled and called me a *tyrant*? We lived through it, though, and you upgraded your standards and I lowered mine. I learned to hold my tongue. When you brought Hank home I eyed him with disdain reserved for earthworms lest you'd see how much I approved! You see, I'd let go when we had the row. And right now I'm going to have to let go again. You know, after this very special baby arrives, you no longer will be "my little girl." You'll have created a whole new generation. So, you see, I guess I'm experiencing just a twinge of jealousy, too.

But, as you say, "momentary," oh, *so* momentary. Actually, I am somewhere up in the ozone layer of delight. This letter, then, is just to say, My Darling, that Mother understands.

You asked that Dad and I help you finish "growing up." We'll all grow up together — up, but not apart. Never!

Oh, yes, about your wedding anniversary. Let's see, that will be six months from next Tuesday, and Baby will be about four weeks old. Of course, we'll sit for you! Bring us a piece of cake, but if you're late, we won't worry. We'll just leave a light on in the hall.

My Mother's Garden

I learned about God in the flowers
In gardens my mother grew —
How He gave seed to the north wind
To plant each time it blew through.

"A miracle, really," she told me,
"That God plans a garden so
Each seed feels a stirring in springtime
To rise when God whispers, 'Grow.' "

It's a beautiful thought Mother taught me —
Old-fashioned, quite "out of date" —
Perhaps, but I've found myself thinking
Of Mother's garden of late. . . .

As I show my children my garden
And nourish each with my prayers,
I know they reach higher toward heaven
With knowledge that Somebody cares.

A Mother's Day Salute

We all have you in common. You are the definite thread that unites the earthly family. You gave us the fragile dream of yesterday, the radiance of today, and the vibrant dreams of tomorrow—in this world and the world to come. You have made a contribution the rest of the world has yet to make; and it will be through your triumphs, your hopes, and your prayers that we will make it. Today is your day. We wish to honor you.

In a world filled with elbows, hurrying feet, and a din of voices, sometimes you must feel pushed aside. Family cords, once so strong, must look fragile. Do you wonder: *Who am I?*

Who are you? In His Sermon on the Mount, Jesus blessed the poor in spirit, they that mourn, the meek, the hungry for righteousness, the merciful, the pure in heart, and the peacemakers. You are all of these. "Ye are the salt of the earth." And we salute you!

Surely you were Theodore Roosevelt's subject in these excerpts: "Into the woman's keeping is committed the destiny of the generations to come after us. . . . In bringing up your children you must remember that while it is essential to be loving and tender, it is no less essential to be wise and firm. Foolishness and affection must not be treated as interchangeable terms. . . . Teach boys and girls alike that they are not to look forward to lives spent in avoiding difficulties; teach them that work, for themselves and for others, is not a curse but a blessing; seek to make them happy, to make them enjoy life, but seek also to make them face life with steadfast resolution, and to do their whole duty before God and to man. Surely she who can thus train her sons and daughters is thrice fortunate among women."

"Of all the commentaries on the Scriptures," wrote John Donne, "good examples are the best." You proved him right.

Carl Sandburg said, "A baby is God's opinion that life should go on." You are proof that it did.

And, so, on this day — *your* day — if you are now called "Mother," be thankful for your unique role in society. If you have a living mother, go thank her for her teaching. And let us all thank the Lord for the older generation from whom we have learned so much. Let us rise to salute them. Blessed are our mothers!

Candles in the Dark

My son lights candles in the dark
And each reveals in part
The little things, not seen or heard,
That lie within my heart.
One candle lights a corner which
I'd thought indeed was bare,
Illuminating some small deed
I'd left forgotten there. . . .
Another candle brings to light
Some incidental word—
So unimportant in itself
I thought it went unheard,
But when repeated back to me
It brings a special glow
As I become acquainted with
The self I did not know. . . .
My son lights candles in my heart
Which make life bright for me—
As in their glow I catch a glimpse
Of a more worthy me.

The Greatest of These

Whatever happens — or matters — in my life leads me to read and reread St. Paul's "Love Chapter." First, I read the King James version, because the language touches the heart of me. Second, I reread it, paraphrasing, according to the needs of the day. It "never fails."

Though I speak several languages with fluency and do not speak lovingly to family, friends, and strangers — the old, the young, the teen-agers, the 'tween-agers — my words have no meaning.

And though I value my education, my familiarity with the classics, and have read all the "great books," I lack understanding unless I study my Bible.

And though I feed every stray cat, donate food to the bake sale, entertain my friends, my son's friends, my and my husband's boss, and have not love, my work brings no satisfaction.

Love never reasons when the family fails to compliment, but continues to match sox, put the cap on the toothpaste tube, bake oatmeal cookies, and read bedtime stories. For love gives itself. It is not bought.

Love does not covet her neighbor's dishwasher or leave her dishes undone because of it and does not call her neighbor to see when she installs a more expensive model. It does not brag when the children excel in school. Neither does it pout when they fail.

Love suffers long when self-pity strikes and does not tell all the neighbors how many remedies have failed.

Love is polite when an anonymous voice notifies her by telephone that the roofing man will be in the neighborhood tomorrow, is patient when the plumbing fails on the day of the family reunion, sees only in part the dirty ring left in the bathtub, and knows that children will grow.

Love never fails, though house plants fade and recipes stop working. God gave me the gifts of faith, hope, and love; and the greatest of these is love. Nothing is going to happen to me today that I am unable to handle through prayer!

Mirrored Memories

Each memory's a looking glass
That all the years reflect—
Lovelier by far, it seems,
When viewed in retrospect.

I Remember Summers

Filled with the sound of porch-screened voices of neighbors come calling, water-sprinkled laughter of children-come-to-play, sad-sweet whine of the fishing line on family camp-outs, dusty-whir of moth wings around the outdoor lanterns, rusty-complaint of the ice-cream freezer, loud sonic boom of firecrackers on Independence Day, followed by the soft muffled-drum music of night birds — all in "turned on" tune.

A Birthday Gift to Remember Me By!

Somewhat eager to impress my child-psychologist friend (I admit in retrospect), I purchased a "proper" gift for her daughter's fourth birthday. Other mothers might choose lethal weapons from *Star Wars* or tooth-decaying "Mr. Wonka's Wonder Bars" from *Charlie and the Chocolate Factory*. But my gift was more acceptable. "Very educational," said the clerk who sold me the Little Miss Kitchen Set: a tiny instant-heat microwave oven (which could not burn small hands), big-print recipes (which mothers could read aloud while performing their own duties), and cake mixes (with fructose — better for the teeth). "A little something to remember me by," I smiled smugly to my hostess.

Well and good. But there was nothing in the book to warn me of what destruction can be wrought by the wrong use of a right gift! The Little Miss was a great hit with the recipient and her guests. One of them plugged the cord in without waiting for help. Another set to mixing a batch of brownies sans directions. All the children wanted to bake at one time. Bedlam broke out, rivaling *Star Wars* and *Charlie and the Chocolate Factory* combined.

As the other mothers cleaned the kitchen and their children, I slunk into a corner and did a bit of "cleaning up" of my own. *Did I honestly have Sonja's good in mind when I chose that gift or was I trying to impress the mother?* One thing was certain: I would be remembered for my "proper" gift, but was it for the "proper" reason? I find it worth thinking about today as I choose gifts for my own child and the children of others . . . "for a gift doth blind the eyes."

Life's Little Things

My heart is content to remember
The treasures of life's little things:
The thrill of a child when it's snowing,
The trill of a bird in the spring.
My heart is content to remember
The worth of each gem in the dews . . .
The circus is here and I'm going . . .
The pride in a new pair of shoes. . . .
My heart is content to remember
Fulfillment that family brings:
The offspring have run my cup over
With pleasure in life's "little things"!

I Thank Her!

For those early years when she sent me to school ready to conquer the world—buttoned in a snowsuit, nourished with hot oatmeal, refreshed with twelve hours of sleep, holding in my hand a clean bill of health from the family doctor, and clutching inside me the warm feeling that she was cheering me on — *I thank her.*

For those middle years when she tried to take my report cards with a grain of salt — taking them as big business, yes, but not falling apart or refusing me the promised slumber party if I failed to earn straight A's — *I thank her.*

For those junior-high-school years when, although she wanted me to become a teacher, she demanded no commitment about a career and recognized that I needed to take my nose out of books long enough to look for hickory nuts and wild persimmons, strum a ukele, and write poetry — *I thank her.*

For those high-school years when she let me breathe, choose my own dresses, and make some decisions on my own, but also made enough demands to keep my mistakes from being the kind that left scars on myself and others — *I thank her.*

For the kind of Christian upbringing that taught *me* to be a better mother, I thank the best mother in the world — my own!

A mother's love! What can compare with it! Of all things on earth, it comes nearest to divine love in heaven.

A mother's love means a life's devotion — and sometimes a life's sacrifice — but one thought, one hope, and one feeling, that her children will grow up healthy and strong, free from evil habits, and able to provide for themselves. Her sole wish is that they may do their part like men and women, avoid dangers and pitfalls, and when dark hours come, trust in Providence to give them strength, patience, and courage to bear up bravely.

Happy is the mother when her heart's wish is answered, and happy are her sons and daughters when they can feel that they have contributed to her noble purpose, and, in some measure, repaid her unceasing, unwavering love and devotion.

—*Anonymous*

After the Easter Service

My pink organdy dress was beautiful! The short skirt was petaled with dainty ruffles that made me look like an inverted rose I thought as I tiptoed to see my reflection before we left for the Easter service. My mother had spent the "egg money" for the materials that year, so eggs would be in short supply. That made no difference. Any sacrifice was worth what I saw of my seven-year-old self in the mirror.

My friends loved the dress so much they just had to feel the fabric (with chocolate-coated fingers I learned later). One little girl, who came home with me to play after church, wanted to try on the new dress. It was too small and she ripped a seam (I learned that later, too). In our rush to get outdoors with our other friends, I hastily hung the beloved dress on a hanger between my heavy winter coat and a raincoat which was badly in need of cleaning.

The Sunday following Easter I ran to get my new dress — only to find it wrinkled, soiled, and ripped. I cried and my mother tried to comfort me, but there was no time to repair the damages before church. Small wonder I spent the worship service observing the wilted lilies somebody had forgotten to water, the cross on the chancel somebody had forgotten to dust, and the faces that many had forgotten to put the smiles of Easter back on.

"What happened to Easter?" I whispered to my mother.

She squeezed my hand in understanding. "Somebody forgot that the Sunday afterward is just as important," she said.

The wee, small incident was great-big in my life. It is important to keep my heart Easter-fresh throughout the year, lest my own child whisper, "But what happened to Easter, Mother?"

Embrace

My arms reach out through time and space
And hold each memory in place:
A creaking swing, a whispered word,
A promise only night winds heard . . .
Bright daffodils in potted clay
And solemn vows we took one day . . .
A little footstep on the stair,
A small, fragmented baby prayer.
My arms reach out through time and space
And do not find an empty place.

A Sky to Share

Though lightning-lit or starry-eyed,
The sky belongs to me
Since—oh, a million nights ago—
I claimed it for my sea
While lying in my bed at night
As cloud-ships floated by
To islands on the Milky Way
Beyond the human eye.
On stormy nights when stars blinked out,
And lightning took their place,
I always knew eventually
My sea would show its face;
Then, playfully, the winds would part
So weary eyes could see
The real estate I knew and loved—
My private property. . . .
And, oh, such loveliness was mine
On calm, untroubled nights
When stars came close to guide my ships
Beyond earth's harbor lights.
I never sold—I never will—
My precious sea of blue
But share it with this child of mine
So he can sail it, too.

Childhood Gone

I thrill to the sounds of children
Laughing at every leap,
By far too much in love with life
To let their parents sleep. . . .
I thrill to the last-blush colors
The sun leaves in its bed
As small children sleep untroubled
Once family prayers are said. . . .
I thrill to memories cherished—
The gentle, lasting kind—
That in their growing and leaving
Small children leave behind.

Star Boarder

He could outsmart me from the day he moved in. What's more, he bragged about it — oh, not verbally, that would be rude — but with looks that saw right through me. It was most disconcerting, but I ignored the signals. After all, I had a household and my sanity to maintain, didn't I? I thought for a while it was a matter of color. Brown eyes were more piercing than my blue ones but not more perceptive. I was wrong, of course — about both.

First, there was the conflict of schedules. "We get up at six, but we'll try not to disturb you," I explained. The faint smile should have prepared me, but I mistook it for agreement. The little bumping sound of his early-morning exercises jarred me awake while it was still dark. "You rest," my husband told me. "I'll speak with him ..." but I doubt if he ever did. The sounds from the smaller bedroom became so regular and rhythmical that I heard them in some faint corner of my dreams.

Second, there was the problem with privacy. We'd always had it in our house-for-two. An extra person should be *un*disruptive. After all, it was *our* house. At first, he stayed put when I talked on the telephone. I spoke in guarded tones, careful not to disturb him. You'd think he would have shown the same consideration, but he began using the exact time for his hobbies—scraping, sawing, hammering. "Don't drive a nail in the wall!" My voice was too shrill, but I was placing an order with Sears.

I should have ignored the hammering I realized too late. "May I borrow your Elmer's glue then?" The pattern was established. He'd tiptoe right past me. "Don't get up," he'd whisper. "I'm just after the Scotch tape . . . the stapler . . . a rubber band."

Third, there was his untidiness! Maybe that was the worst of it all. Where I used to tidy up once a day I found myself spending more time in what had once been the spare bedroom than I spent on the rest of the entire house. What's more, I found the borrowed items in never-dreamed-of places like shoe boxes, bird cages, and under the bed. It was underneath the bed that I found things I *didn't* know he'd borrowed—a screwdriver, my Revlon lipstick, clothespins, a box of iron-on patches, and the vaporizer!

"Look," I said, "we have to talk. . . ." His large, brown eyes were liquid with remorse. "I'm sorry—truly. I meant to put them all back. . . ." And he did, trip after trip—banging the door just when I was trying to hear the weather report or take down a recipe. "QUIET!" Later I had to apologize, of course. He always put me in the wrong, even when I knew I wasn't. "It's all right," he'd soothe, and I'd feel worse.

I hadn't realized I was counting and adding up the score against him until it came to the food thing. "The fourth problem is the meal situation," I complained to my husband. "Do you realize how many hours my kitchen's open for business?"

But I never should have taken my husband's sugges-

tion about letting him eat with us now and then. One meal led to another. Then we were never alone. His table manners were disgraceful, which meant I'd have to work hard at setting a fine example or get a plastic tablecloth. In the end, I did both. He was so *clumsy*!

Overtired and irritable, I scolded him and nagged my husband. "It's his age, honey," indulgently as one speaks of the little-and-helpless or the old-and-infirm.

And both of them would pat me, leaving oatmeal fingerprints on my arms and little indentations of guilt in my heart. Tomorrow, *tomorrow,* I would be more patient. But he mistook my change for softness and gave every indication of staying permanently and taking over completely. No more leisurely breakfasts. No more candlelight dinners. Mealtime was his to do with as he chose — so gently and so subtly I wouldn't have known how to prevent it even had I seen it happening. "You'll want to see my rock collection . . ." and sand sifted into the salad. "Oops! Sorry about the spaghetti. Should I wipe it with my napkin or call the cat?"

"I got a sore knee at the ball park. Maybe a Band-Aid when you've finished that roll. I told a fellow I met at the park he could call me at mealtime — he was a little lonely. Oh, there's the car horn — the whole basketball team, I guess. Is there some of the yummy chocolate cake left and just a little Coke? If the phone rings while I'm away. . . .

While he's away! I used to let it ring, because I knew it would ring again. But now I answer it. Once I didn't say, "Hello," just, "Your rent's overdue." And he said soothingly, "I don't live there anymore. Remember?"

Yes, I remember. Nobody tiptoes past while I'm talking on the phone.

"Hamburgers tonight —" I'd promise him anything, *anything* — this wonderful, this perfect son who was never a minute's trouble.

"Would it be too much bother — ?"

Just wait till I tell my husband our star boarder is coming home! And my cup overflows.

Gladness

I have not sought out foreign places:
There's gladness in familiar faces
Who share with me from year to year
The lovely things they see and hear . . .
The gladness in a Sunday meal;
The rhythm of a turning wheel;
The goodness of the golden rule;
Some lesson learned in Sunday school;
A hawthorn bud, a summer's rain;
The waving of September grain;
The trusting hands of tiny tots
Or playing ball in vacant lots;
An invitation someone sent
When birthdays were a big event;
The gladness of a sunset view
Or roses wet with morning dew;
The power of a raging sea;
An answered prayer, a memory. . . .
One need not travel far
When gladness lies where children are.

Think of it this way: Children are a tax-exempt investment in happiness.
And this way: No investment, no return!

Getting to Know You (Again)

One of the nicest gifts those of us who are blessed with husbands in the home can give our children is a warm, loving relationship with their father. Yes, there are times when mothers must be child-centered, but any good thing can go a smidgen too far. So there comes a day when the man in our lives reminds us of his prior claim. We are pleased and flattered that he wants us to go on that weekend business trip or for a three-day spin "just to be alone." Pleased and flattered, but, "What can we do about the children?"

Well, there are grandparents, two sets of them if you are lucky.

There are your after-school neighbors who "looked in" on the too-big-for-a-sitter child or established "sitters" who might help.

There are licensed care centers which take in a limited number of children for short periods, and there are families who "adopt" a child as a family member while parents are away.

A recent and highly favored program is that of "parent surrogates." These people are generally seniors — sea-

soned parents who have coped with just about all life's "little problems." Sometimes they will take children into their homes. Others prefer to come into the children's familiar territory.

Are there uncles and aunts who can swap "services"? This works especially well if they have cousins for your flock to enjoy. Be prepared to offer them the same service.

Then, there are friends who might appreciate exchanging a sitting service. Contemporary parents can juggle four sometimes more easily than two what with the joy of school-let-out and the age-old question, "What can we do now?"

There are high dividends for your "getting away." You will come home refreshed after your renewed courtship and be "dying" to see the children who were "driving you wild" a few days earlier! The children will have accumulated a tan and a new sense of responsibility. Great strides in the mental health of all.

There are a few sensible precautions and then you are off! Have whatever physical checkups your child or children may be in need of before your departure. Leave instructions for any medication any of your family may need to take. Also leave a copy of your itinerary and emergency numbers at which another member of the family can be reached should you be unavailable.

If your children balk at the idea of Mother and Daddy leaving them, all of you need this vacation very much!

Would you become an instant millionaire? Laugh more often today than you laughed yesterday. Give some part of yourself away. Forgive each person who offends you. Reach out to meet a new friend. Pray for an enemy. Smell a rose. And hold a newborn baby in your arms.

Happiness

God sends children for another purpose than merely to keep up the race — to enlarge our hearts; to make us unselfish and full of kindly sympathies and affections; to give our souls higher aims; to call out all our faculties to extended enterprise and exertion; and to bring round our firesides bright faces, happy smiles, and tender hearts.

My soul blesses the great Father every day that He has gladdened the earth with little children.

—Mary Howitt

Christmas began with a gift from God. It was meant to be shared! God's gift was anticipated. Anticipate Christmas with your family.

Give Roses for Christmas

Look out of doors. Are the roses in bloom? Then it is time to gather them from your garden to make into sweet-smelling gifts for Christmas. You will need loads of petals, so get the children to help, for "rose hunting" is lots of fun. You see, the blooms should be picked carefully every morning after the dew has dried. Roses like to be picked. The more you pick them, the better they grow and bloom. Just be kind as you cut them from the stems. First, learn exactly how to pick and store the blossoms. Then read how to prepare them for the beautiful dried flower presents that will perfume the entire house when the lid is taken from each jar. And, yes, you will learn how to prepare the jars, too.

Cut the flowers from the rose bushes very carefully so you will hurt neither the plant nor yourself. It is good to wear gloves to protect your hands. Clip roses with scissors or shears as you would for a bouquet. Next, carefully pull each petal from the blossoms that are opened wide and throw away the thorny stems. Save some green leaves in a separate pile and now and then clip and save a tiny, unopened bud. Foil trays from TV dinners work well to keep the petals, leaves, and buds separated. Handle the flowers gently for you want them to hold their shape for decorating after they are "cured."

Do you have an old window screen? A piece of screen, butcher paper, or even newspaper will work in a pinch. Keep the collection out of the sun during the drying process, out of the way so it won't be walked on and crushed, and propped on rocks so the wind can get underneath to help dry petals, leaves, and buds. Cover with wax paper if your collection is in a drafty place.

Drying takes awhile. If you use screen, turn the petals two or three times a week (this makes a fun assignment for one or several family members). If using paper, turn the petals each day so the air can circulate beneath them. Encourage rose hunting daily (in your garden or a friend's) and add to the collection. Each time a new batch is started, use a separate screen or paper. Dating batches is helpful (another fun assignment).

While the roses are drying, look around for other flowers: violets, poppies, daisies, anything that will press neatly. Place these between pages of old magazines and weight them down with rocks. Children can do all of these jobs — half the fun!

You'll need large glass jars. Mayonnaise and pickle containers are fine — the larger the better for you will be adding each new batch of petals as they cure. Petals will lose their bright color when exposed to light, so keep them stored in a dark closet or wrap newspaper around the jars after putting petals inside.

Sometimes it takes petals only three or four days to dry. Others will take as long as two weeks. You can tell when the petals are ready by lifting (Careful! They'll crumble!). They should be lightweight and look like colored cornflakes.

Now, with some of the blossoms dried and stored in a dark place and still others drying, it is time to begin searching for small jars in which to put each little gift arrangement. Look for odd-shaped jars like those that hold pimento peppers, spices, etc. The jars should be small, but not so small that you cannot get fingers part way in because decorating is the next step. Carefully remove the pressed flowers from the magazine together with the green rose leaves and buds. You will need white glue, too. Use a toothpick dipped in the glue for picking up the pressed violet or bud. With another toothpick, put a little glue on each petal. Place each flower or bud against the inside of the jar. The job is easier if the jar is lying flat. Now put your finger inside the jar and carefully press the flower in place. Add a leaf the same way. As you practice all sort of imaginative ideas will evolve — adding a leaf here, a bud there. Set the decorated containers away and go back to the cured petals. You are ready to "spice" them to make them smell doubly sweet!

Choose spices from the kitchen. Experiment with cinnamon, nutmeg, mace, pieces of dry orange peel, or crumbled vanilla bean. Pour the dry rose petals on wax paper in separate piles and add only one spice to each pile. About one-fourth teaspoonful sifted over the petals will spice two or three cups of dried flowers.

The last step is to lift the spiced petals (trying to keep them whole) and put them into the decorated containers. Be careful not to disturb the design on the inside. Working slowly is the secret, and you will need to caution eager children. Last of all, tie with gay ribbons and keep hidden until Christmas as a sweet-scented surprise for relatives and friends — your very own special blend of "frankincense and myrrh."

The promise of resurrection is written on every leaf that grows.

—author unknown

A Surprise in an Egg Shell!

Children love to "grow" things. Easter is an ideal time to grow something. Every blade of grass is straining heavenward.

You are busy with church programs, spring mother-and-daughter style shows, and seventeen are coming to Easter Sunday dinner. So, let the children do this little project on their own. Get them started by breaking eggs, (use yolks and whites later in the hot-cross buns), at the little end. With very little help, the children can break off little pieces from each shell until it is down to about half its original size. Suggest that they smooth the edges carefully with an emery board or a nail file. Color the shells with watercolor or tempera; or, if you have none on hand, rub the shells with crepe paper dipped in a small amount of water. Each shell should be a different shade. Top ruffling is easy to do. A little white glue will hold a scrap of lace in place. Or bind the top of the shells by applying the glue to the edge and using pieces of leftover colored braid, bias tape, or ribbon.

Now, for the gift box: spray paint an egg carton gold or silver or suggest that the children color the carton in the same manner they colored the egg shells. The gift box is as practical as it is pretty, for it will serve as a little greenhouse for growing an Easter gift for a special person.

Demonstrate how to put a bit of soil into each shell (being careful to keep the decorated "pots" clean). Pots are now ready for planting with a flower or vegetable seed. Water according to directions on the seed package. No matter what the climate, plants can be grown indoors, ready for outdoor planting when the weather conditions are right. Another good feature about this method of starting a garden is that plants need not be disturbed when transplanting. Just "plant" pot and all. Shells will dissolve.

A Search for "The Windows of Gold"

Nobody talked about "the generation gap" when I was growing up. My mother was much more concerned with what she called "common sense" in handling problems. Looking back on it now I realize she recognized a certain gap between my problems and her attempts to solve them, and she resorted to her own mother's wisdom. It was a "sensible" thing to do. There was then, is now, and always will be, I think, a wider gap between Mama's thinking and mine than Grandma's and mine. Either my mother knew about the gap or she was so busy with the endless tasks only mothers know about that she was happy to hand me over to my grandmother. "*Grandma* has time for me," I used to say accusingly. "Of course, she has," my mother would agree, "so let her handle some of the little things."

One of the "little things" on one particular day had to do with my hair, which I thought my mother should do something about. Another was my eyes which I was sure *nobody* could do anything about. And so I was desperate. I was tearing at my drab (I thought) bangs and screwing up my eyes because they didn't look at all like the movie star I was going to be when Grandma came in. She inspected me carefully, and I knew that my mother had prepared her for one of my moods.

"Let's see now," she said slowly, picking up a hair-brush. "No problem about the sheen. A hundred strokes will do it. Now, the eyes you'll have to handle. The shine comes from inside."

The latter part I didn't understand, of course—not then anyway. But I understood about the hair. I watched my brown hair pick up burnished lights as Grandma brushed and told me a story called "The Windows of Gold."

What may have been a recognition of the narrower gap between grandparent-grandchild than between mother-daughter (or a neat dodge on Mama's part!) gave me some needed ammunition in dealing with my own son later. Over and over I repeated the story always ending with my grandmother's tacked-on moral: "It is far more important to put a sheen into your own life than to waste time coveting the possessions of others."

Once upon a time there was a small boy with a man-sized dream. Each morning at sunrise he looked from the front window of his cabin high on a mountaintop into the gold-filled windows of a great cathedral in the valley below. Some day, surely, his legs would be strong enough for him to travel the long distance so that he could get a better view.

At last he could wait no longer. "But," those around him protested, "you should wait until the winter is past."

No, he could not wait. Indeed! It was the promised warmth in the golden windows below which begged him to begin his search.

All day the child traveled down the rugged mountain-side. He was cold and hungry. His shoes were worn thin. None of this mattered for ahead of him the welcoming beams reached out to guide his steps—until suddenly the light went out!

The small boy looked in dismay, realizing that he had reached the valley just at sundown. He called out to a stranger. "Please, sir," he begged. "Can you help me? I have lost my guiding light. Can you show me where the golden windows are?"

The stranger touched the child's outstretched hand gently. "It is dark here in the valley," he said. "You must look to the mountaintop for the windows of gold."

The boy turned to raise his eyes above the trail he had traveled. And there, in his very own front window high above, the last rays of the setting sun reflected. "I need not have searched," said the small boy in amazement as he looked at the distant window of his own home.

I loved that story. As a matter of fact, I grew to appreciate my drab hair because of it! One hundred strokes a day would do the trick, but I doubled the count just for good measure. "Why, my hair is beautiful," I said in awe to my grandmother one day. And both of us smiled understandingly. I had found the sheen in my own ordinary hair that I'd envied in the hair of another. When the realization came, I was sitting in the glow of the setting sun in Grandma's parlor.

Many years later, I learned the meaning of the shine of the eyes. I guess my mother and my grandmother knew that discovery takes maturity. Happy eyes shine. And even not-so-happy eyes can shine if we let them. In shining we reflect a "golden window" for somebody in the valley before the sun is up or on the cold peaks where the sun has moved out of sight.

I wonder just how many times grandmothers have been the "golden windows" that busy mothers need?

Children are God's apostles, sent forth, day by day, to preach of love, and hope, and peace.

—*J. R. Lowell*

A Mother Talks to God

Dear Lord, You have gifted me with children and I am humbly grateful, but

I need Your wisdom to deal with my children gently but firmly as I ought.

As they look up to me for guidance, I must look up to you. Shape me, O Lord, into the kind of model I should be.

Let me assume this task unselfishly. Let me enrich their lives rather than expecting them to enrich my own.

Where there are mountains, let me climb—knowing that small feet are following. And let my shadow be short, that they may climb in the sunlight of Your love.

Put a bridle on my tongue lest I nag, scold, belittle, or embarrass.

Let me not compare these little ones with one another—either favorably or unfavorably—but lead them to know that they are individuals created in Your perfect image.

Keep my heart and my mind open to new ideas so that I may not be in conflict with their desires when, later,

they must choose. Rather, let me work at strengthening family ties.

Make my life a shining example of the golden rule.

Let me share the wisdom of my years lovingly and be a gentle learner in the new pasture of their learning as well.

Let me double—even triple—the love I give my children, but let me love them with my eyes wide open.

If I am blinded in my love, I will be unable to coach them when coaching is needed.

Let me temper my discipline with love, knowing that there is strength in restraint.

Loving them as I do, Lord, I will need Your help when the time comes for us to part. Prepare me to let them go when their wings are strong, and strengthen my wings that I may share them with You in the mansions of eternity.

Amen.

A mother's love is indeed the golden link that binds youth to age; and he is still a child, however time may have furrowed his cheek or silvered his brow, who can yet recall, with softened heart, fond devotion or gentle chidings of the best friend that God ever gives us.

—Bovee

I Think God Knew

I think God knew that children
Had need of both their hands
And they could use two others
(With heart that understands);
It had to be a someone
Whose voice was low and sweet
To soothe a crying baby,
Someone with tireless feet. . . .
I think God knew that children
Would need a great, big smile
Which said each time they stumbled,
"You'll make it after while."
Someone who'd read them stories
And know each childhood game,
Then point to constellations
And give each star a name. . . .
I think God knew the nation
Had need of wisdom shared
By older generations
Who'd passed this way — and cared . . .
And so He fashioned mothers
With gentle, loving grace
And gave them hearts of angels
With a human face.

Face to Face

The garden that I grew this year
Took such a little space;
And yet 'twas there between its rows
I met God face to face.
One cannot walk a garden path —
Or so it seems to me —
And watch the bulbs, like children, grow
And miss eternity;
For life goes on (God showed me there)
With rebirth every year;
And I will travel on like them
When I have bloomed right here.
So now I touch each Queen Anne's Lace
In my waiting place.
For it was there between its rows
I met God face to face.

Stories Do Come True!

My mother always read to me
The stories she liked best,
Of kings and queens, old magic lamps,
And how we won the West.
We journeyed far on flying rugs
As Mother read to me;

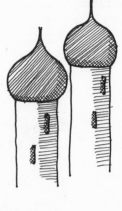

We walked on every foreign shore
And charted every sea.
We traveled by the stars at night,
On wings of wind by day;
Our road map was her storybook—
We never lost our way.
Oh, there were poems, too, of course,
And Bible stories old
About the miracles of Christ
And cities paved in gold.
I've never met a dragon yet,
I guess I never will;
And there's no need, if such there be,
To scale a steep glass hill.
And yet there's purpose in my life,
Imagination, too,
Put there by stories read to me . . .
So, really, they "came true."

Granola Logs

Surprise the children with a "log rolling" party. Fun, easy to do, good, and so good for them!

1 cup of dry (powdered) milk

½ cup strained honey

½ cup peanut butter

1 cup granola or other "natural grain" cereal

1. Mix all ingredients together and roll into a "log" about eighteen inches long and one inch in diameter.
2. Roll log in dry granola (as much as will stick).
3. Wrap log in waxed paper and put in refrigerator or freezer.
4. Cut into thin slices and serve about thirty friends.
5. From this basic recipe, you can lead the children to create recipes of their own under your supervision. They might try using less honey and adding other sweet flavors: a bit of maple syrup or molasses, dried apricots or figs or dates, even a squeeze from a fresh orange. They can vary the log "rolling" by using wheat germ, toasted coconut, or crushed nuts (preferably unsalted), such as almonds, pistachios, peanuts, or sunflower seeds.